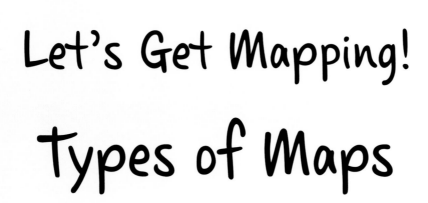

Let's Get Mapping!

Types of Maps

Melanie Waldron

Chicago, Illinois

Edited by Nancy Dickmann and Abby Colich
Designed by Victoria Allen
Original illustrations © 2013
Illustrated by HL Studios
Picture research by Ruth Blair
Originated by Capstone Global Library Limited
Printed and bound in China by CTPS

17 16 15 14
10 9 8 7 6 5 4 3 2

**Library of Congress Cataloging-in-Publication
Data**
Waldron, Melanie.
  Types of maps / Melanie Waldron.
     p. cm.—(Let's get mapping!)
  Includes bibliographical references and index.
  ISBN 978-1-4109-4904-2 (hb)—ISBN 978-1-4109-
  4911-0 (pb) 1. Maps—Juvenile literature. I. Title.
  GA105.6.W352 2013
  912—dc23   2012008819

Acknowledgments

We would like to thank the following for
permission to reproduce photographs:
Alamy: pp. 6 (© fStop), 19 (© imagebroker);
iStockphoto: pp. 10 (© Samuel Kessler),
21 (© Emrah Turudu); Shutterstock: pp. 5 (© Noel
Powell, Schaumburg), 7 (© Alfonso de Tomas),
13 (© djgis), 14 (© Tyler Olson), 20 (© algabafoto),
22 (© Pichugin Dmitry); Superstock:
pp. 4 (© Cultura Limited), 11 (© age fotostock)
25 (© Photononstop), 26 (© Fotosearch);
Wellcome Library, London: p. 17.

Cover photograph of a GPS over a paper map
is reproduced with permission from Shutterstock
(© Pincasso).

Background images and design features
reproduced with permission from Shutterstock.

Every effort has been made to contact
copyright holders of any material reproduced
in this book. Any omissions will be rectified
in subsequent printings if notice is given to
the publisher.

All the Internet addresses (URLs) given in this
book were valid at the time of going to press.
However, due to the dynamic nature of the
Internet, some addresses may have changed,
or sites may have changed or ceased to exist
since publication. While the author and
publisher regret any inconvenience this may
cause readers, no responsibility for any such
changes can be accepted by either the author
or the publisher.

Contents

Some words appear in the text in bold, **like this**. You can find out what they mean by looking in the glossary.

What Is a Map?

When you think of a map, you might think of a flat piece of paper. It will show some **symbols**. These are little pictures or shapes that represent things in real life. For example, a white square with a red cross on it might represent a hospital.

A map is a way of showing information about the land. There are many different types of maps that can show different types of information. There could be many maps of one area, each one showing different information.

Skiers use **trail maps** to find the correct route down a mountain. This can prevent them from getting lost or skiing off a steep cliff!

What are maps used for?

Maps help people travel around and find places. They can be used to learn about different places and how people live there. Maps can also be used to help us explain things—for example, the weather.

Sailors use maps of the sea floor to avoid hitting rocks and sandbanks under the water.

PAPERLESS MAPS

Today, many people use digital maps. These are maps that you can see on a screen, such as a computer or cell phone. There are millions of online maps available on the Internet.

Round Earth, Flat Map

Earth is not flat! Our planet is a **sphere**, like a ball. The most accurate map of Earth is called a **globe**. It can spin around so that you can see where all the countries are. A globe really helps us to see the position of each country and **continent** on Earth.

Although globes are very useful, there are some problems with using them. They are difficult to carry around and store. They cannot be used in books, and they usually cost a lot more than flat paper maps.

Globes can show us where countries, continents, and oceans are located on Earth.

Flattened Earth

Flat paper maps can be carried around or used as part of books and newspapers. When we use flat maps, we have to imagine that Earth has been crushed flat. **Cartographers** (people who make maps) have clever ways to do this.

A flat map uses something called a **projection** to make it flat. There are different kinds of projections. Each one squeezes Earth in a different way.

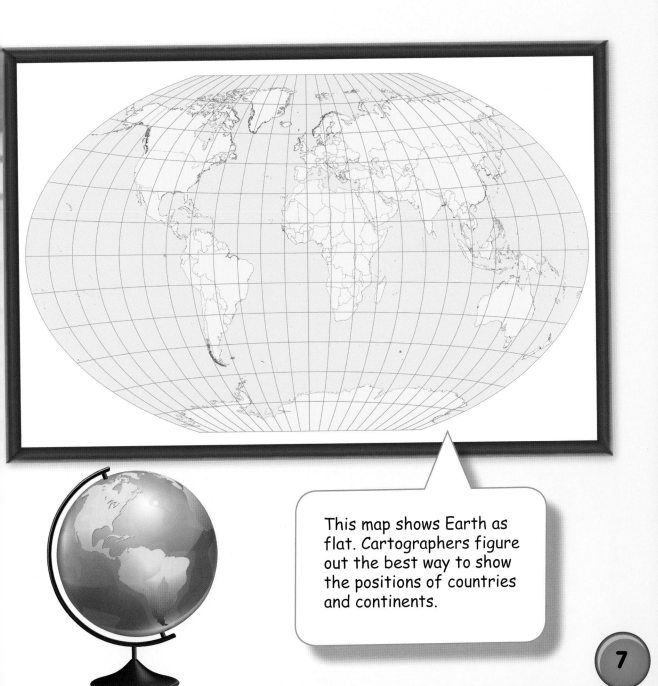

This map shows Earth as flat. Cartographers figure out the best way to show the positions of countries and continents.

Political and Physical Maps

Political maps show areas of land and their **borders**. Borders are imaginary lines that separate things. International borders separate countries. Different states, counties, or regions inside countries have borders to separate them.

Many borders are simply lines on a map. Sometimes a **natural feature** such as a river can be a border. Often, there is nothing in real life to show where borders are.

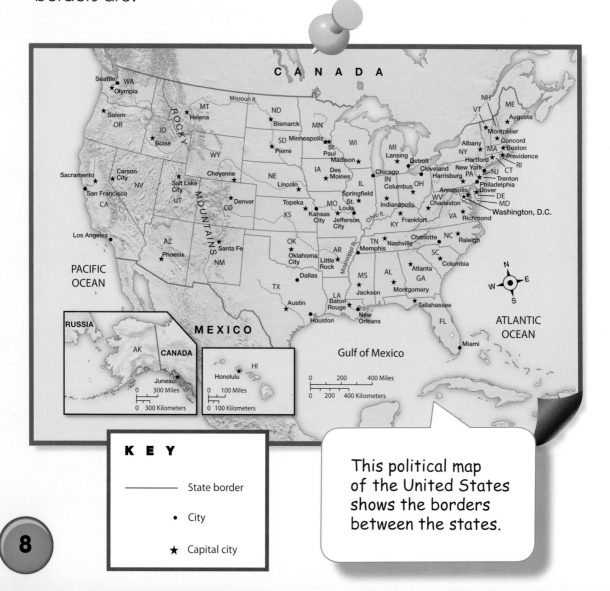

This political map of the United States shows the borders between the states.

K E Y

————— State border

• City

★ Capital city

Physical maps

Maps that show the shape of the land are called **physical maps**. They also show natural features such as rivers and lakes. They show areas that are flat and areas that are hilly or mountainous. Many physical maps also show the borders between countries, and some show buildings and roads.

This is a physical map of the United States.

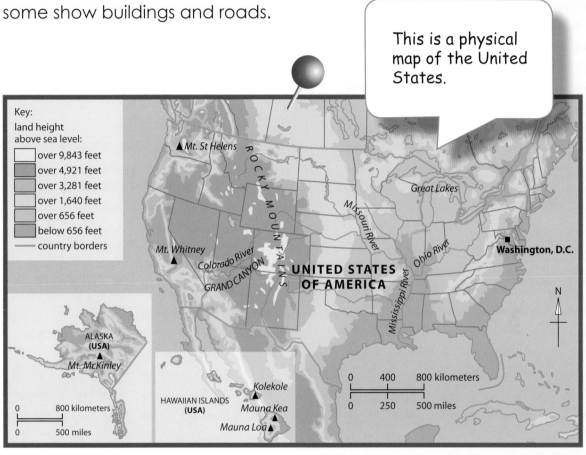

Key:
land height above sea level:
- over 9,843 feet
- over 4,921 feet
- over 3,281 feet
- over 1,640 feet
- over 656 feet
- below 656 feet
- country borders

▲ Mt. St Helens

ROCKY MOUNTAINS

Great Lakes

Missouri River

Mt. Whitney ▲

Colorado River

GRAND CANYON

UNITED STATES OF AMERICA

Mississippi River

Ohio River

Washington, D.C. ■

N

ALASKA (USA)

Mt. McKinley ▲

HAWAIIAN ISLANDS (USA)

Kolekole ▲

Mauna Kea ▲

Mauna Loa ▲

0   800 kilometers
0   500 miles

0   400   800 kilometers
0   250   500 miles

DIVIDING PEOPLE

Some of the international borders in Africa were created by European governments in the 1800s. The border between Kenya and Tanzania was created in 1890. This split up an area called Maasailand, where the Maasai people had lived together for thousands of years.

Transportation Maps

Many countries have lots of roads. Most people need road maps to help them drive around the country. Detailed road maps have almost all roads marked on them. They also show cities, towns, and villages.

Road maps need to show twists and turns in the roads. All the roads need to follow the same direction as in real life. This is to help drivers figure out where they are and where they need to go.

On this road map of San Antonio, Texas, major highways in the downtown area are shown in blue. Other important roads are shown in orange and yellow.

Railroads

Countries with railroads need maps to help people plan their train journeys. Railroad maps do not need to show the twists and turns of the railroad lines. This means that railroad maps can sometimes look very different from the real-life railroad lines.

This map shows the routes of the New York City subway system, or MTA. It shows the subway lines as mostly straight, with the stations evenly spaced out.

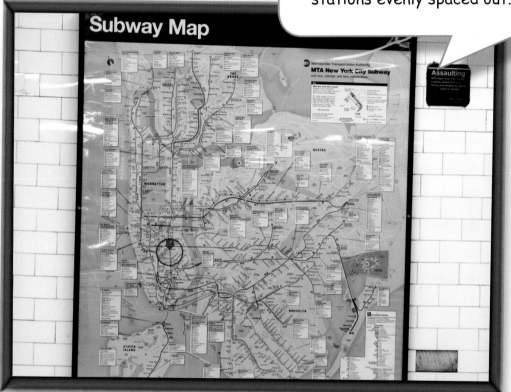

GPS

GPS is short for "global positioning system." Many modern cars have GPS devices. These show digital maps on a small screen and tell the driver where to go. Many drivers no longer use paper road maps.

Weather and Topography

Weather maps are useful for showing us what the weather in our area is like. **Weather forecast** maps show us what the weather might be like over the next few days. Weather maps show very little information about what is on the land. They usually just show some towns and cities, to help us know which area we are looking at.

This weather forecast map shows what the weather will be like in the United States.

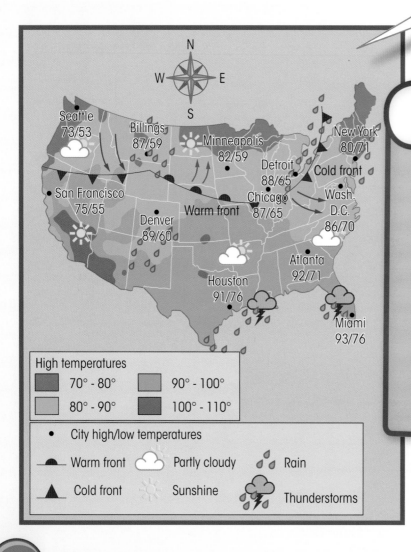

CHANGING MAPS

Weather maps are always changing! They use different symbols to show us how the weather is changing and what type of weather we should expect. Online maps can be updated several times a day as weather forecasters update their forecasts.

Land details

Topographical maps show huge amounts of detail about the land's surface. They usually have **contour lines** to tell us how high the land is and how steep or flat it is. A contour line runs along all the land at the same height. Contour lines spaced far apart tell us that the land is quite flat. Contour lines packed closely together tell us that the land is very steep.

Topographical maps give us very detailed information about the shape of the land.

Land Use and Resources

Making maps of the way the land is used can help us to understand many things about an area. A land-use map of Nepal, a mountainous country, would show that large areas are used for tourism and conservation.

Land-use maps can use symbols to show different types of land use. They can also use different colors to represent different land uses. There are lots of different land uses, including farming, housing, and transportation.

A land-use map of the United States will show that huge areas are used for growing cereal crops.

Mapping resources

Resource maps can show us the important resources of an area, such as coal, oil, and diamonds. People use maps to figure out the best places to explore for these things.

Resource maps can also include things like wind. Energy can be captured using windmills, so it is useful to know where windy places are.

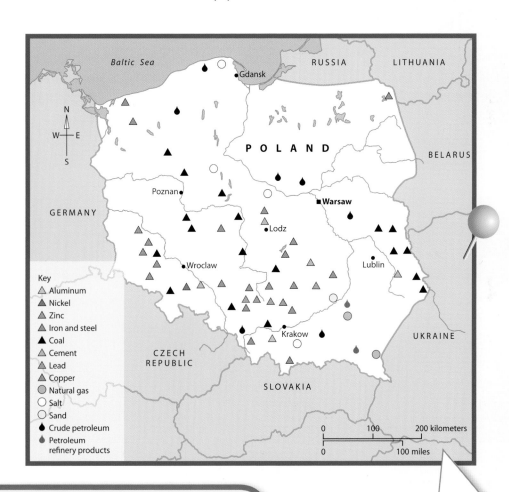

Key
△ Aluminum
▲ Nickel
△ Zinc
△ Iron and steel
▲ Coal
△ Cement
△ Lead
△ Copper
⚪ Natural gas
⚪ Salt
⚪ Sand
🌢 Crude petroleum
🌢 Petroleum refinery products

This is a resource map of Poland. It shows where some valuable resources can be found.

PRECIOUS WATER

Fresh water is a very precious resource in many areas of the world. It is becoming more important to map water—even underground water resources—so that it can be used wisely and protected from pollution.

Statistical Maps

Many maps show information about countries and the people living there. Statistical maps show **statistics**. Statistics are numbers. All kinds of numbers can be represented on a map.

Statistical maps can show information in different ways. Different sizes of symbols could show different numbers of things. For example, a small circle could show all villages with fewer than one thousand people. A large circle could show cities with over one million people.

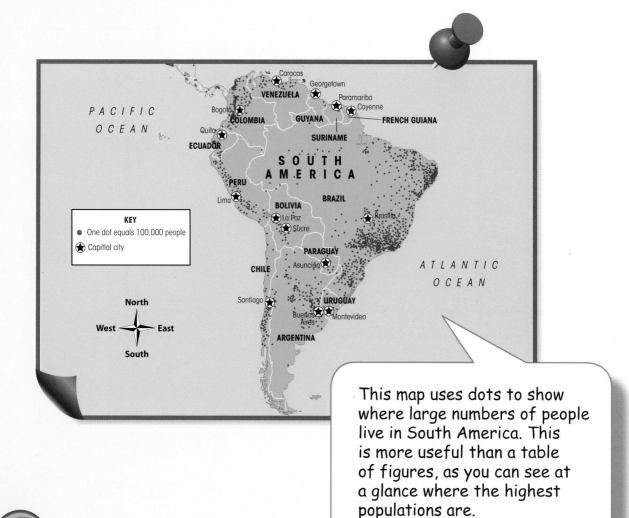

KEY
- One dot equals 100,000 people
- ⭐ Capitlal city

North
West — East
South

This map uses dots to show where large numbers of people live in South America. This is more useful than a table of figures, as you can see at a glance where the highest populations are.

Different statistics

A world map could show the average temperature for each country. A map of a country could show the percentage of people over the age of 60 in each city. A map of a town could show the number of people living in each house.

MYSTERY DISEASE

John Snow was a doctor living in London, England, in the 1800s. He marked on this map where people with a disease called **cholera** lived. He used the map to figure out where the cholera was coming from—a nearby water pump. The pump handle was removed, and the cholera cases decreased.

Tourist Maps and Town Maps

Maps of your local area show small areas of land. They can show lots of detail about the land—far more detail than a world map or country map could show. These maps are called large-scale maps. Maps that show much less detail, but cover a much larger area, are called small-scale maps.

Large-scale maps of a town or city can be really useful. They can include street names to help us find places and addresses. They can use symbols to show important buildings. They can also show where bus stops and bus routes are.

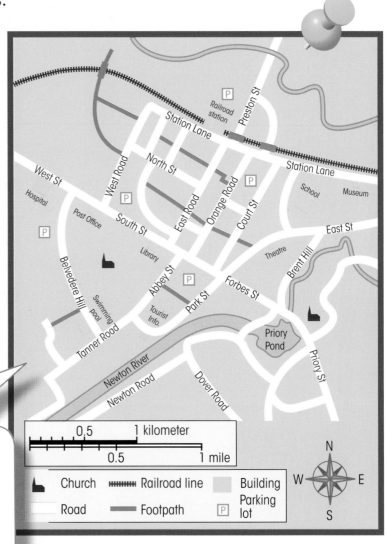

This is a large-scale map of a town's downtown area. Some of the streets are named, and some locations have symbols.

Pictorial maps

Some areas that have lots of visiting tourists have special tourist maps. These show the things that might be interesting for tourists—museums, restaurants, and hotels, for example. Some towns or parks use **pictorial maps**. These maps show tiny drawings of the buildings and attractions. Pictorial maps are fun to look at and make it easier for tourists to find things.

This pictorial map shows downtown Elche, Spain. There are little drawings of some of the buildings.

19

Historical Maps, Modern Maps

People have been making and using maps for hundreds of years. Many of the first maps were made by explorers who were sailing to new places. Often, they made their maps from sketches of the areas they explored.

PRINTING MAPS

Until the 1400s, maps had to be hand-drawn and copied by hand. This made them very rare and also very expensive. During the 1400s, printing machines were invented. This meant that copies of maps could be made, and more people could own them.

Modern maps

Today, most maps are made using **aerial photographs** and **satellite images**. Aerial photographs are taken by cameras fitted to airplanes. Satellites can take very detailed photographs of Earth's surface.

Surveyors help cartographers by checking the land at ground level. They make sure that the aerial photographs and satellite images are accurate. They also provide information that cartographers cannot tell from photographs—for example, street names and building types.

Many modern maps are digital and are displayed on screens instead of being printed on paper.

Same Place, Different Map

In this book, you have seen that there are many different kinds of maps. They all contain different information and they are all used for slightly different purposes. This means that any one area could have lots of different maps, all showing different things.

A map of this area could show that very few people live here, or how the land is used.

Mixing information

Sometimes it is useful to see a mix of different kinds of information on a map. This means that we can try to explain patterns. For example, a map showing where people live around the world would show areas of high and low population. If you added information about the world's weather to this map, you would see that there are very few people where the weather is usually very cold or very hot and dry.

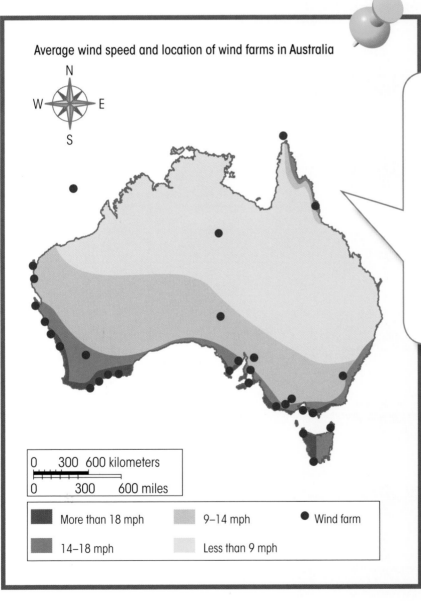

Average wind speed and location of wind farms in Australia

This map shows the location of wind farms and the average wind speeds, in Australia. Most of the wind farms are where the average wind speed is highest.

0   300 600 kilometers

0   300   600 miles

More than 18 mph   9–14 mph   ● Wind farm

14–18 mph   Less than 9 mph

Reading Maps

Reading a map is a very useful skill. It can help you travel around and find places. If you can read a map, you can also find out some really useful information about places.

> If you had to follow the trail on this map, it would be helpful if you knew how to read the map!

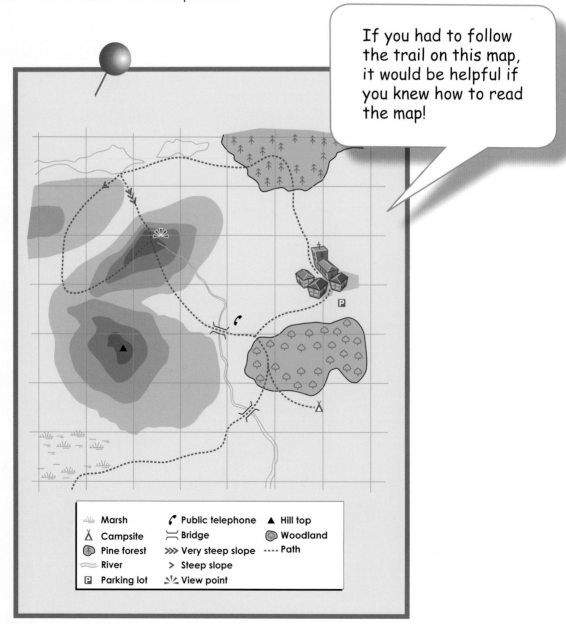

Marsh		Public telephone		Hill top	
Campsite		Bridge		Woodland	
Pine forest		Very steep slope		Path	
River		Steep slope			
Parking lot		View point			

Important map-reading skills

No matter what type of map you are looking at, some basic skills are important. First, always check the map's title. Then you will know what the map is trying to show you.

Most maps have a **compass rose** printed on them, showing which way is north, south, east, and west on the map. Use a compass to make sure you have the map turned the right way up, so that it matches north, south, east, and west in real life.

To help you figure out distances in real life, use the **bar scale** on the map. This is a line or bar with numbers printed on it. If you measure the distance you want to know about and then hold this against the bar scale, you can figure out the distance.

Street maps can help you to walk around places without getting lost.

Space Maps

There are some maps that do not show any part of Earth at all—maps of space! The first maps of the Moon were made in the 1960s, to see if it would be possible to land a spaceship on it. NASA, the U.S. space agency, has also made maps of Mars, Mercury, Venus, and the moons of Jupiter and Saturn.

The Hubble Space Telescope was launched in 1990. It sends amazing images of space back to Earth.

Mapping the sky

Maps of the night sky, as seen from Earth, have been used for hundreds of years. Sailors used them to help them sail their ships in the right direction. Night sky maps show the planets that are near Earth. They also show stars that are incredibly far away.

Maps of the night sky are different for different locations around the world. The night sky also changes as Earth turns. This means that you must make sure you are looking at the correct night sky map for your area. Once you have the correct map, you can start to name the stars and planets you can see.

Night sky maps show the stars and planets that are visible from Earth.

NORTH

CASSIOPEIA

CEPHEUS

URSA MINOR

THE BIG DIPPER
(PART OF URSA MAJOR)

DRACO

DELPHINUS

CYGNUS

HERCULES

BOOTES

EAST

WEST

LYRA

CORONA BOREALIS

AQUILA

SERPENS CAPUT

LIBRA

SERPENS CAUDA

OPHIUCHUS

SAGITTARIUS

SCORPIUS

SOUTH

Get Mapping!

Look at these three maps. They show the same area, but they show different information about the area.

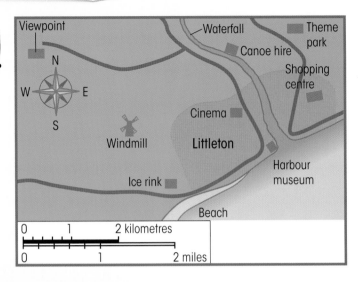

A

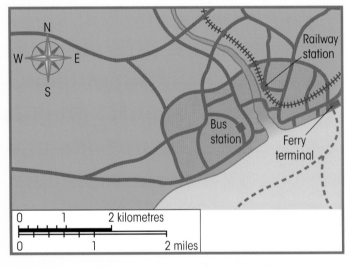

B

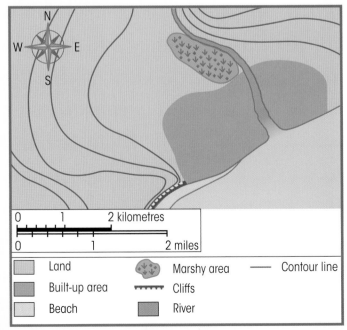

C

	Land		Marshy area		Contour line
	Built-up area		Cliffs		
	Beach		River		

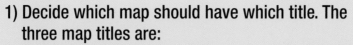

1) Decide which map should have which title. The three map titles are:

- Littleton Area Transportation Networks and Terminals
- Littleton Area Tourist Features
- Littleton Area Topography

2) Which map would you use if you were planning a long walk in the country?

3) Which map would you send to friends who were planning to visit the town?

4) Which map would be useful for a business that wanted to transport its goods?

5) Imagine you wanted to add more information to one of the maps. For example, you could add some weather information. Choose the map you think would be the best one to use. You could trace it and add weather information to it. Why did you choose that map? Who might want to know about the weather? Would they have chosen the same map as you?

Glossary

aerial photograph photograph taken from high above Earth's surface, usually from an airplane

bar scale bar or line on a map that shows you how far a distance on the map represents in real life

border imaginary line that separates different countries or different regions inside a country

cartographer person who makes maps

cholera dangerous infectious disease that causes stomach cramps and sickness

compass rose drawing with four points, showing where north, south, east, and west are on a map

continent one of Earth's seven major areas of land: North America, South America, Europe, Africa, Asia, Australia, and Antarctica

contour line line that follows all the land at a certain height above sea level

globe round ball with a map of Earth on it

natural feature something on Earth's surface that has been created by nature—for example, a mountain

physical map map that shows the shape of the land and its natural features

pictorial map map that has tiny drawings of the features it wants to show; it is often used in popular tourist places

political map map that shows countries and their borders, and often capital cities

projection way of displaying an image on a screen or flat area

resource something of value to humans that Earth can provide

satellite image picture, like a photograph, that a satellite can take of Earth from space

sphere solid, round object

statistic number that gives information about something

symbol object or a picture that represents something

trail map map of the ski runs and ski lifts in a ski area

weather forecast weather that is likely to happen in a place in the near future

Find Out More

There is a whole world of maps and mapping waiting to be discovered! Try looking at some other books and some web sites to get you started.

Books

Challoner, Jack. *The Atlas of Space*. Brookfield, Conn.: Copper Beech, 2001.

Jackson, Kay. *Types of Maps* (Ways to Find Your Way). Mankato, Minn.: Capstone, 2008.

Johnson, Jinny. *Maps and Mapping* (Inside Access). Boston: Kingfisher, 2007.

Torpie, Kate. *Maps Types* (All Over the Map). New York: Crabtree, 2008.

Web sites

education.nationalgeographic.com/education/multimedia/ interactive/maps-tools-adventure-island/kd/?ar_a=3
Play this interactive game to learn more about how symbols on a map work.

www.nationalatlas.gov
This U.S. government web site offers many different kinds of maps of the United States, such as maps that show different types of land, weather, and the number of people living in an area.

www.nationalgeographic.com/kids-world-atlas/maps.html
This National Geographic page is full of links to information about maps. The resources listed here will help you create your own maps, zoom in on different parts of the world, and much more!

weather.gov
This is the web site for the National Weather Service. Look at maps with different kinds of forecasts throughout the country.

Index